# R Data Preparation and Manipulation Using the sqldf Package

Executing SQL Statements from Within R Program

Djoni Darmawikarta

Copyright © 2017 by Djoni Darmawikarta

# Table of Contents

Acknowledgements ................................................................... 2

Introduction .............................................................................. 4

    Introducing sqldf ................................................................ 4

    Database Options ............................................................... 8

Chapter 1: Sub-setting a Data Frame ..................................... 10

    Selecting Columns ............................................................ 10

    Selecting Rows ................................................................. 11

    Selecting All Columns ...................................................... 12

        All Columns with Specific Order ................................. 12

    Compound Conditions ..................................................... 13

    Evaluation Precedence and the Use of Parentheses ........... 14

    NOT logical operator ....................................................... 15

    BETWEEN Operator ....................................................... 16

    IN Operator ...................................................................... 16

    LIKE Operator ................................................................. 17

    Escaping the Wildcard Character ..................................... 17

    Combining the NOT operator .......................................... 19

    Handling NULL ............................................................... 19

Chapter 2: Manipulating a Data Frame .................................. 22

    Renaming Column ........................................................... 22

    Expression ........................................................................ 22

    DISTINCT Keyword ....................................................... 23

    Aggregate Functions ........................................................ 26

    CASE expression .............................................................. 26

| | |
|---|---|
| Simple CASE | 26 |
| Searched CASE | 28 |
| Ordering Output Rows | 29 |
| WHERE Presence | 32 |
| Storing the Subset Output | 32 |
| Chapter 3: Grouping and Aggregating Rows | 34 |
| GROUP BY Clause | 34 |
| HAVING Keyword | 36 |
| Chapter 4: Joining Multiple Data Frames | 40 |
| Data Frame Aliases | 41 |
| Joining on More than One Column | 43 |
| Left Outer Joins | 44 |
| Absence of rows in one of data frames | 45 |
| Self-Joins | 45 |
| Natural Joins | 46 |
| Chapter 5: Merging Output Data Frames | 50 |
| UNION ALL | 51 |
| UNION | 51 |
| INTERSECT | 52 |
| EXCEPT | 53 |
| Chapter 6: Built-in Functions | 54 |
| Numeric Functions | 54 |
| ABS | 54 |
| ROUND | 54 |
| SIGN | 55 |
| Character Functions | 56 |

- SUBSTR ............................................................. 56
- LOWER and UPPER ........................................... 56
- LENGTH ............................................................ 57
- Datetime Functions ................................................... 57
- CURRENT_DATE ............................................... 57
- Null related functions ............................................... 58
- Chapter 7: Oracle Database ............................................. 62
- Create Data Frame from Database ............................. 62
- Full Outer Joins ......................................................... 63
- STDDEV Function ..................................................... 64
- Analytics Windowing .................................................. 64
- DML Statements ........................................................ 65
- Index .............................................................................. 68

## Acknowledgements

Thanks to the R Core Team and G. Grothendieck.

R Core Team (2015). **R**: A language and environment for statistical computing. R Foundation for Statistical Computing, Vienna, Austria. URL http://www.R-project.org/.

G. Grothendieck (2014). **sqldf**: Perform SQL Selects on R Data Frames. R package version 0.4-10. http://CRAN.R-project.org/package=sqldf

# Introduction

Welcome to *R Data Preparation and Manipulation Using the sqldf Package*. This book shows you how to use SQL within R using the sqldf package. You will learn, by examples, the sqldf package and SQL. You will need some R skills to follow the examples.

SQL (Structured Query Language) is the standard language of database, e.g. SQLite and Oracle, which we cover both in this book.

sqldf is an R package, which allows you to use SQL statements, SELECT statement in particular, to manipulate R data frames.

## Introducing sqldf

When you load the sqldf package, the RSQLite package is also loaded.

```
> library(sqldf)
Loading required package: gsubfn
Loading required package: proto
Loading required package: RSQLite
```

A SQLite database, which is an embedded relational database, is built in the RSQLite package.

The sqldf package has one function only, the sqldf function. The SQL statement(s) is one of the arguments of the function. The "sqlstatements" is mandatory.

```
sqldf("sqlstatements", …)
```

When the function is called, the connected SQLite database engine executes the SQL statements. A copy of the data frames you specify on the statement are created in the SQLite database. The data copy will be dropped (removed) from database when the execution is completed.

Here is an example session to demonstrate what happens. First, we create a data frame named product by loading it from a product.csv file.

```
> product <- read.csv("D:/product.csv",
      na.strings="")
```

The product data frame now is available in our workspace.

```
> product

  p_code    p_name launch_dt price
1      1      Nail 31-3-2017    10
2      2    Washer 29-3-2018    15
3      3       Nut 29-3-2018    15
4      4     Screw 30-3-2020    25
5      5 Super Nut 30-3-2021    30
6      6   New Nut              NA
```

**Note:**

The output has the row numbers on the very first column this is not a column of the data frame, it's just the way R displays a data frame. If you need to, you can suppress the row numbers using the print function and set its row.names argument = FALSE, as follows.

```
> print(product, row.names=FALSE)

 p_code    p_name launch_dt price
      1      Nail 2017-01-31    10
      2    Washer 2017-01-29    15
      3       Nut 2017-01-29    15
      4     Screw 2017-01-30    25
      5 Super_Nut 2017-01-30    30
      6   New Nut              NA
```

We now open a connection to the SQLite database by calling the sqldf function without any argument.

```
> sqldf()

<SQLiteConnection>
  Path: :memory:
  Extensions: TRUE
```

Next, we call the sqldf function to query the product data frame. We would like to read the rows for p_code greater than 2. Note that the SQL statement is not case sensitive. (I usually wrote the SQL reserved words in uppercases other words in lowercases. I will use this style in this book).

```
> sqldf("SELECT * FROM product WHERE p_code > 2")

  p_code    p_name  launch_dt price
1      3       Nut 2017-01-29    15
2      4     Screw 2017-01-30    25
3      5 Super Nut 2017-01-30    30
4      6   New Nut               NA
```

The function returns a data frame (the query's output), a subset of the customer data frame.

```
> class(sqldf("SELECT * FROM product WHERE p_code > 2"))
[1] "data.frame"
```

Behind the scene a product data frame is created in the connected SQLite database and the product data is copied. We can query the product table on the database, where the SQLite table name is prefixed with main.

```
> sqldf("SELECT * FROM main.product ")
  p_code     p_name launch_dt price
1      1       Nail 2017-01-31    10
2      2     Washer 2017-01-29    15
3      3        Nut 2017-01-29    15
4      4      Screw 2017-01-30    25
5      5  Super Nut 2017-01-30    30
6      6    New Nut               NA
```

When we disconnect from the SQLite database, the main.customer data frame is no longer available.

```
> sqldf()

NULL

> sqldf("select * from main.product")

Error in rsqlite_send_query(conn@ptr, statement) :
  no such table: main.product
```

Of course the customer data frame is still available in our workspace.

```
> sqldf("select * from product")
  p_code     p_name launch_dt price
1      1       Nail 2017-01-31    10
2      2     Washer 2017-01-29    15
3      3        Nut 2017-01-29    15
4      4      Screw 2017-01-30    25
5      5  Super Nut 2017-01-30    30
6      6    New Nut               NA
```

If we do not explicitly open a SQLite connection, when we call the sqldf function, a connection is established and disconnected transparently (automatically), and the main.product table is no longer available.

```
> sqldf("select * from product")

  p_code    p_name  launch_dt price
1      1      Nail 2017-01-31    10
2      2    Washer 2017-01-29    15
3      3       Nut 2017-01-29    15
4      4     Screw 2017-01-30    25
5      5 Super Nut 2017-01-30    30
6      6   New Nut               NA

> sqldf("select * from main.product")
Error in rsqlite_send_query(conn@ptr, statement) :
  no such table: main.c_order
```

## Database Options

The SQL statement you specify on the sqldf function is executed by the connected database SQL engine. The SQLite database is the default. The SQL statements must be supported by (conform to the SQL) by the database in use. If you need to execute an SQL statement on another database installed and connected. Chapter 7 shows some examples using Oracle database.

## Chapter 1: Sub-setting a Data Frame

In this chapter you will learn how to subset a data frame. You will learn how to work on multiple data frames in Chapter 4. You create a subset of a data frame using a SELECT statement.

Here's the SELECT statement syntax.

```
SELECT selectlist FROM dataframe [WHERE condition]
```

- The WHERE clause is optional. Without it all rows will be in the output data frame.

### Selecting Columns

The *selectlist* lists the columns you want in the output data frame. You write the columns in the sequence you want them in the output data frame.

Let's say we have the following product data frame.

```
> product

  p_code      p_name  launch_dt price
1      1        Nail 2017-01-31    10
2      2      Washer 2017-01-29    15
3      3         Nut 2017-01-29    15
4      4       Screw 2017-01-30    25
5      5   Super Nut 2017-01-30    30
6      6     New Nut               NA
```

In the following example, the selectlist is p_name (product name) and price columns.

```
> sqldf("SELECT p_name, price FROM product ")

    p_name   price
1     Nail     10
2   Washer     15
3      Nut     15
4    Screw     25
5 Super Nut   30
6  New Nut    NA
```

## Selecting Rows

To select specific rows, you use the WHERE clause. Only rows that satisfy the WHERE condition will be in the subset. The SELECT statement in the following sqldf selects only rows having price equal to 15.

```
> sqldf("SELECT p_name, price FROM product WHERE
    price = 15 ")
  p_name price
1 Washer    15
2    Nut    15
```

The <= in the above WHERE condition is one of the comparison operators. Here are the list comparison operators you can use.

| Operator | Description |
| --- | --- |
| = | Equal to |
| < | Less than |
| > | Greater than |
| <= | Less than or equal to |
| >= | Greater than or equal to |
| != | Not equal to |

The following example uses the != operator. The output data frame has all but the Nut product.

```
> sqldf("SELECT p_name, price FROM product WHERE
    p_name != 'Nut' ")

    p_name price
1     Nail    10
2   Washer    15
3    Screw    25
4 Super Nut   30
5  New Nut    NA
```

## Selecting All Columns

You can specify * in the SELECT clause to pull all columns as in the following example.

```
> sqldf("SELECT * FROM product WHERE p_name !=
    'Nut'")

  p_code   p_name  launch_dt price
1      1     Nail 2017-01-31    10
2      2   Washer 2017-01-29    15
3      4    Screw 2017-01-30    25
4      5 Super Nut 2017-01-30   30
5      6  New Nut                NA
```

## All Columns with Specific Order

If you want a specific order of the columns on the subset output, you need to specify the columns in the order you want.

```
> sqldf("SELECT p_name, p_code, price, launch_dt FROM
    product WHERE p_name != 'Nut' ")

    p_name p_code price  launch_dt
1     Nail      1    10 2017-01-31
2   Washer      2    15 2017-01-29
3    Screw      4    25 2017-01-30
4 Super Nut     5    30 2017-01-30
5  New Nut      6    NA
```

## Compound Conditions

The condition p_name != "Nut' in the previous example is called a predicate. Using the AND and OR logical operator you can combine predicates to form a compound condition. Only rows that satisfy the compound condition will be returned by the query.

The rules for the OR logical operator are as follows.

| Left condition | Logical operator | Right condition | Compound condition |
|---|---|---|---|
| True | OR | True | True |
| True | OR | False | True |
| False | OR | True | True |
| False | OR | False | False |

In principle, the result of the OR compound condition is true (satisfying the condition) if any one of the two conditions being OR-ed is true otherwise, if none of the conditions is true, the compound condition is false (not satisfying the condition).

The rules for the AND logical operator are as follows.

| Left condition | Logical operator | Right condition | Compound condition |
|---|---|---|---|
| True | AND | True | True |
| True | AND | False | FALSE |
| False | AND | True | FALSE |
| False | AND | False | FALSE |

Basically, the result of the AND compound condition is true only if the two conditions being AND-ed are true otherwise, the result is false.

The following example contains three predicates in its WHERE clause.

```
> sqldf("SELECT * FROM product
+       WHERE (DATE(launch_dt) >= DATE('2017-01-31')
+       OR price            > 15)
+       AND (p_name        != 'Nail') ")
  p_code   p_name launch_dt price
1      4    Screw 2017-01-30    25
2      5 Super_Nut 2017-01-30    30
```

The result of the first compound condition (launch_dt >= '2017-01-30' OR price > 15) is true for Nail, Screw and Super_Nut rows in the product data frame AND-ing this result with the (p_name != 'Nail') predicate results in two products, the Screw and Super_Nut.

Note that New Nut does not satisfy the condition because applying any of the comparison operators to NULL results in false (the price and launch_dt of the New Nut are NULL). The section "Handling NULL" later in this chapter explains more about NULL.

## Evaluation Precedence and the Use of Parentheses

If a compound condition contains both the OR condition and the AND condition, the AND condition will be evaluated first because AND has a higher precedence than OR. However, anything in parentheses will have an even higher precedence than AND.

The previous SELECT statement has an OR and an AND, but the OR condition is in parentheses so the OR condition is evaluated first. If you remove the parentheses in the SELECT statement, the query will return a different result.

```
> sqldf("SELECT * FROM product
+       WHERE DATE(launch_dt) >= DATE('2017-01-31')
+       OR price            > 15
+       AND (p_name         != 'Nail') ")

  p_code   p_name  launch_dt  price
1      1     Nail 2017-01-31     10
2      4    Screw 2017-01-30     25
3      5 Super Nut 2017-01-30    30
```

Without the parentheses, the compound condition price > 15 AND p_name != 'Nail' will be evaluated first, resulting in the Screw and Super_Nut. The result is then OR-ed with the launch_dt >= 2017-01-31' condition, resulting in these three rows.

## NOT logical operator

You can use NOT to negate a condition and return rows that do not satisfy the condition.

Thanks to the NOT operator, the two rows not satisfying the condition in will now be returned.

```
> sqldf("SELECT * FROM product
+       WHERE NOT (DATE(launch_dt) >= DATE('2017-01-31')
+       OR price            > 15
+       AND (p_name         != 'Nail')) ")

  p_code p_name  launch_dt  price
1      2 Washer 2017-01-29     15
2      3    Nut 2017-01-29     15
```

Here's another example where we negate the last predicate only (as opposed to the previous query that negated the overall WHERE condition).

```
> sqldf("SELECT * FROM product
+       WHERE DATE(launch_dt) >= DATE('2017-01-31')
+       OR price            > 15
+       AND NOT (p_name     != 'Nail') ")
```

```
  p_code p_name launch_dt price
1      1   Nail 2017-01-31    10
```

## BETWEEN Operator

The BETWEEN operator evaluates equality to any value within a range. The range is specified by a boundary, which specifies the lowest and the highest values.

Here is the syntax for BETWEEN.

```
SELECT columns FROM dataframe
WHERE column BETWEEN(lowest_value, highest_value)
```

The boundary values are inclusive, meaning *lowest_value* and *highest_value* will be included in the equality evaluation.

The following BETWEEN operator to specify the lowest and highest prices that need to be returned.

```
> sqldf("SELECT * FROM product WHERE price BETWEEN 15
   AND 25 ")

  p_code p_name launch_dt price
1      2 Washer 2017-01-29    15
2      3    Nut 2017-01-29    15
3      4  Screw 2017-01-30    25
```

## IN Operator

The IN operator compares a column with a list of values. The syntax for a query that uses IN is as follows.

```
SELECT columns FROM data frame
WHERE column IN(value1, value2, ...)
```

The following IN operator to select all columns whose price is in the list (10, 25, 50).

```
> sqldf("SELECT * FROM product WHERE price IN (10,
    25, 50) ")

  p_code p_name  launch_dt price
1      1   Nail 2017-01-31    10
2      4  Screw 2017-01-30    25
```

## LIKE Operator

The LIKE operator allows you to specify an imprecise equality condition. The syntax is as follows.

```
SELECT columns FROM data frame
WHERE column LIKE ' ... wildcard_character ... '
```

The wildcard character can be a percentage sign (%) to represent any number of characters or an underscore (_) to represent a single occurrence of any character.

The following LIKE operator finds products whose name starts with N and is followed by two other characters plus products whose name starts with Sc and can be of any length.

```
> sqldf("SELECT * FROM product WHERE p_name LIKE
    'N__' OR p_name LIKE 'Sc%' ")

  p_code p_name  launch_dt price
1      3    Nut 2017-01-29    15
2      4  Screw 2017-01-30    25
```

Even though you can use LIKE for numeric columns, it is primarily used with columns of type string.

## Escaping the Wildcard Character

If the string you specify in the LIKE operator contains an underscore or a percentage sign, SQL will regard it as a wild character. For example, if you want to query products that have an underscore in their names, your SQL statement would look like the following.

```
SELECT * FROM product WHERE p_name LIKE '%_%'
```

Assume our product data frame is as follows. It has a Super_Nut, with the underscore.

```
> product

  p_code    p_name  launch_dt  price
1      1      Nail 2017-01-31     10
2      2    Washer 2017-01-29     15
3      3       Nut 2017-01-29     15
4      4     Screw 2017-01-30     25
5      5 Super_Nut 2017-01-30     30
6      6   New Nut                NA
```

When you execute the following sqldf, you will get all rows instead of just the Super_Nut, because the underscore in the LIKE operator is regarded as a wild card character, i.e. any one character.

```
> sqldf("SELECT * FROM product WHERE p_name LIKE
       '%_%' ")

  p_code    p_name  launch_dt  price
1      1      Nail 2017-01-31     10
2      2    Washer 2017-01-29     15
3      3       Nut 2017-01-29     15
4      4     Screw 2017-01-30     25
5      5 Super_Nut 2017-01-30     30
6      6   New Nut                NA
```

The following resolves the problem by prefixing the wild card character with an ESCAPE character. In the statement the ESCAPE clause defines ^ as an escape character, meaning any character in the LIKE operator after a ^ will be considered a character, not as a wildcard character. Now only rows whose p_name contains an underscore will be returned.

```
> sqldf("SELECT * FROM product WHERE p_name LIKE
    '%^_%' ESCAPE '^' ")

  p_code     p_name launch_dt price
1      5  Super_Nut 2017-01-30    30
```

## Combining the NOT operator

You can combine NOT with BETWEEN, IN, or LIKE to negate their conditions.

```
> sqldf("SELECT * FROM product WHERE price NOT
    BETWEEN 15 AND 25 ")

  p_code     p_name launch_dt price
1      1       Nail 2017-01-31    10
2      5  Super_Nut 2017-01-30    30
```

## Handling NULL

NULL, an SQL reserved word, represents the absence of data. NULL is applicable to any data type. It is not the same as a numeric zero or an empty string or a 0000/00/00 date.

The result of applying any of the comparison operators on NULL is always NULL. You can only test whether or not a column is NULL by using the IS NULL or IS NOT NULL operator.

Our product data frame has New Nut row with NA in its price. (NA is equivalent to NULL).

```
> product

  p_code     p_name launch_dt price
1      1       Nail 2017-01-31    10
2      2     Washer 2017-01-29    15
3      3        Nut 2017-01-29    15
4      4      Screw 2017-01-30    25
5      5  Super_Nut 2017-01-30    30
6      6    New Nut               NA
```

The following = NULL produces no subset output.

```
> sqldf("SELECT * FROM product WHERE price = NULL ")
[1] p_code    p_name    launch_dt price
<0 rows> (or 0-length row.names)
```

To get the New Nut use IS NULL as follows.

```
> sqldf("SELECT * FROM product WHERE price IS NULL")

  p_code  p_name launch_dt price
1      6 New Nut              NA
```

## Chapter 2: Manipulating a Data Frame

The columns of the output subset do not need to be just the columns from the source data frame.

### Renaming Column

By default the names of the output columns in the query output are the names of the columns of the data frame. You can give them different names or aliases if you wish.

The syntax for the SELECT clause that uses aliases is as follows.

```
SELECT column_1 AS alias1, column_2 AS alias2, ...
FROM dataframe
```

An alias can consist of one or multiple words. In the following example we give the p_name column an alias "PRODUCT NAME".

```
> sqldf("SELECT p_code, p_name AS 'PRODUCT NAME' FROM
    product ")

  p_code PRODUCT NAME
1      1         Nail
2      2       Washer
3      3          Nut
4      4        Screw
5      5    Super_Nut
6      6      New_Nut
```

### Expression

An output column can be an expression. An expression in the SELECT clause can include columns, literal values, arithmetic or string operators, and functions. Two of the following query's output columns are arithmetic expressions.

```
> sqldf("SELECT price, (price * 0.1) price_increase,
     (price + price * 0.1) new_price FROM product")

  price price_increase new_price
1    10            1.0      11.0
2    15            1.5      16.5
3    15            1.5      16.5
4    25            2.5      27.5
5    30            3.0      33.0
6    NA             NA        NA
```

**DISTINCT Keyword**

A query may return duplicate rows. Two rows are duplicates if each of their columns contains exactly the same data. If you don't want to see duplicate output rows, use DISTINCT in your SELECT clause. You can use DISTINCT on one column or multiple columns.

## Using DISTINCT on A Single Column

Here's again our product data frame.

```
> product
  p_code    p_name  launch_dt price
1      1      Nail 2017-01-31    10
2      2    Washer 2017-01-29    15
3      3       Nut 2017-01-29    15
4      4     Screw 2017-01-30    25
5      5 Super_Nut 2017-01-30    30
6      6   New Nut               NA
```

The following applies DISTINCT to one column, the price column.

```
> sqldf("SELECT DISTINCT price FROM product ORDER BY
        price ")
  price
1    NA
2    10
3    15
4    25
5    30
```

Without DISTINCT, the query in will return six rows that include two duplicate prices, the 15.

```
> sqldf("SELECT price FROM product ORDER BY price ")
  price
1    NA
2    10
3    15
4    15
5    25
6    30
```

## Using DISTINCT on Multiple Columns

If a query returns multiple columns, two rows are considered duplicates if all their columns have the same values. They are not duplicates if only one column has the same value.

The DISTINCT keyword can be applied on multiple columns too.

In the following example, output rows with the same price and launch_dt will be in the output subset once only.

```
> sqldf("SELECT DISTINCT price, launch_dt FROM
    product ORDER BY price ")

  price  launch_dt
1    NA
2    10 2017-01-31
3    15 2017-01-29
4    25 2017-01-30
5    30 2017-01-30
```

Here's an example of the use of the UPPER built-in function on the output column.

```
> sqldf("SELECT UPPER(p_name) new_price FROM
    product")

  new_price
1      NAIL
2    WASHER
3       NUT
4     SCREW
5 SUPER_NUT
6   NEW_NUT
```

## Aggregate Functions

You can manipulate your query output further by using aggregate functions. The aggregate functions are listed here.

| Function | Description |
| --- | --- |
| MAX(column) | The maximum column value |
| MIN(column) | The minimum column value |
| SUM(column) | The sum of column values |
| AVG(column) | The average column value |
| COUNT(column) | The count of rows |
| COUNT(*) | The count of all rows including NULL. |

Here's an example using the aggregate functions.

```
> sqldf("SELECT MAX(price),
+    MIN(price),
+        SUM(price),
+        AVG(price),
+        COUNT(price),
+        COUNT(*)
+        FROM product
+        ")
  MAX(price) MIN(price) SUM(price) AVG(price) COUNT(price) COUNT(*)
1         30         10         95         19            5        6
```

Note that **only COUNT(*)** takes into account the New Nut product the other functions do not as its price is NULL.

## CASE expression

CASE allows you to have dynamic query output in which a column value may vary depending on the value of the column. CASE comes in two flavors: Simple and Searched. Both will be explained in the following subsections.

### Simple CASE

The general syntax for the Simple CASE is as follows.

```
SELECT columns,
  CASE column
    WHEN equal_value1
    THEN output_value1
    WHEN equal_value2
    THEN output_value2
    WHEN ...
    [ELSE else_value]
  END AS output_column
FROM dataframe
WHERE ...
```

In the Simple CASE, *column_name* is compared to *equal_value*s in the WHEN clause, starting from the first WHEN and down to the last WHEN. If *column_name* matches a WHEN value, the value right after the THEN clause is returned and the CASE process stops. If *column_name* matches none of the WHEN values, *else_value* is returned if there exists an ELSE clause. If *column_name* matches none of the WHEN values but no ELSE clause exists, NULL will be returned.

In the following an example, the query uses a Simple CASE expression for the price column to produce a price_cat (price category) output column.

```
> sqldf("SELECT p_code,
+    p_name,
+         CASE price
+         WHEN 10
+         THEN 'Cheap'
+         WHEN 15
+         THEN 'Medium'
+         WHEN 25
+         THEN 'Expensive'
+         ELSE 'Others'
+         END AS price_cat
+         FROM product ")
  p_code    p_name price_cat
1      1      Nail     Cheap
2      2    Washer    Medium
3      3       Nut    Medium
4      4     Screw Expensive
5      5 Super_Nut    Others
6      6   New_Nut    Others
```

## Searched CASE

The case in the Simple CASE compares a column with various values. On the hand, the case in the Searched CASE can be any condition. Here is the syntax for the Searched CASE.

```
SELECT columns,
  CASE
    WHEN condition1
    THEN output_value1
    WHEN condition2
    THEN output_value2
    WHEN ...
    ELSE else_value
  END AS output_column
FROM dataframe
WHERE ...
```

The conditions are evaluated starting from the first WHEN and down to the last WHEN. If a WHEN condition is met, its THEN output_value is returned to the output_column and the CASE process stops. If none of the WHEN conditions is met, *else_value* is returned if there exists an ELSE clause. If no condition is met and no ELSE clause exists, NULL will be returned.

In the following example, the query uses a Searched CASE. While the Simple CASE example categorized the products based on only their prices, this Searched CASE categorizes the products based on the various conditions involve more than just the price.

```
> sqldf("SELECT p_code,
+   p_name, price, launch_dt,
+       CASE
+       WHEN (price <= 10
+       AND p_name NOT LIKE 'Nut%')
+       THEN 'Cheap'
+       WHEN price BETWEEN 11 AND 25
+       THEN 'Medium'
+       WHEN price > 25 and DATE(launch_dt, 'YYYY-MM-
          DD') > DATE('20170329', 'YYYY-MM-DD')
+       THEN 'Expensive'
+       WHEN price IS NULL
+       THEN 'Not valid'
+       ELSE 'Others'
+       END AS product_cat
+       FROM product ")

  p_code    p_name price  launch_dt product_cat
1      1      Nail    10 2017-01-31       Cheap
2      2    Washer    15 2017-01-29      Medium
3      3       Nut    15 2017-01-29      Medium
4      4     Screw    25 2017-01-30      Medium
5      5 Super_Nut    30 2017-01-30      Others
6      6   New Nut    NA             Not valid
```

## Ordering Output Rows

You can order output rows based on certain criteria using the ORDER BY clause. The ORDER BY clause must appear last in a SELECT statement.

Here is the syntax for a query having the ORDER BY clause.

```
SELECT columns FROM dataframe
WHERE condition ORDER BY column(s)
```

## Ordering by One Column

To order your query output rows, use the ORDER BY clause with one column.

```
> sqldf("SELECT p_code, p_name FROM product ORDER BY
      p_name ")

  p_code    p_name
1      1      Nail
2      6   New Nut
3      3       Nut
4      4     Screw
5      5 Super_Nut
6      2    Washer
```

## Direction of Order

The default direction is ascending. To order a column in descending direction, use the DESC reserved word.

```
> sqldf("SELECT p_code, p_name FROM product ORDER BY
      p_name DESC ")

  p_code    p_name
1      2    Washer
2      5 Super_Nut
3      4     Screw
4      3       Nut
5      6   New Nut
6      1      Nail
```

## Multiple Columns

To order by more than one column, list the columns in the ORDER BY clause. The sequence of columns listed is significant. The order will be conducted by the first column in the list, followed by the second column, and so on. For example, if the ORDER BY clause has two columns, the query output will first be ordered by the first column. Any rows with identical values in the first column will be further ordered by the second column.

```
> sqldf("SELECT * FROM product ORDER BY launch_dt,
    price ")

  p_code    p_name launch_dt price
1      6   New Nut              NA
2      2    Washer 2017-01-29   15
3      3       Nut 2017-01-29   15
4      4     Screw 2017-01-30   25
5      5 Super_Nut 2017-01-30   30
6      1      Nail 2017-01-31   10
```

## Different Directions on Different Columns

You can apply different order directions on ordered columns too. The output rows will be ordered by launch_dt in ascending order and then by price in descending order. Now, the Super_Nut comes before the Screw.

```
> sqldf("SELECT * FROM product ORDER BY launch_dt
    ASC, price DESC ")

  p_code    p_name launch_dt price
1      6   New Nut              NA
2      2    Washer 2017-01-29   15
3      3       Nut 2017-01-29   15
4      5 Super_Nut 2017-01-30   30
5      4     Screw 2017-01-30   25
6      1      Nail 2017-01-31   10
```

## WHERE Presence

If your SELECT statement has both the WHERE clause and the ORDER BY clause, ORDER BY must appear after the WHERE clause.

```
> sqldf("SELECT * FROM product WHERE p_name = 'Nut'
+ ORDER BY p_name, p_code DESC ")
  p_code p_name  launch_dt price
1      3    Nut 2017-01-29    15
```

## Storing the Subset Output

You can of course keep the subset output in a data frame.

```
> example.subset <- sqldf("SELECT * FROM c_order
      WHERE c_no > 2 ")

> example.subset

  order_no c_no p_code qty order_dt
1        5    3     30  90 2017-1-2
2        6    4     40 100 2017-1-2
3        7    4     45 110 2017-1-2
```

## Chapter 3: Grouping and Aggregating Rows

A group is a set of rows having the same value on specific columns. In the previous Chapter 2 you learned how to apply aggregate functions on all output rows. In this chapter you learn how to create groups and apply aggregate functions on those groups.

### GROUP BY Clause

If your query has a WHERE clause and ORDER BY clause, a GROUP BY clause must appear after the WHERE clause and before the ORDER clause.

Here is the syntax for a SELECT statement with the WHERE, GROUP BY, and ORDER BY clauses.

```
SELECT columns,
   aggregate_function(group_columns)
FROM dataframe
WHERE condition
GROUP BY group_columns
ORDER BY column(s)
```

Here's the product data frame again, for your easy reference.

```
> product
  p_code    p_name  launch_dt price
1      1      Nail 2017-01-31    10
2      2    Washer 2017-01-29    15
3      3       Nut 2017-01-29    15
4      4     Screw 2017-01-30    25
5      5 Super_Nut 2017-01-30    30
6      6   New Nut               NA
```

In the following example, the query groups the output from the product data frame by their launch date. Aggregations will be done by the four grouped launch dates: 29, 30 and 31 of March 2013, and NULL.

```
> sqldf("SELECT launch_dt,
+ MAX(price) ma,
+ MIN(price) mi,
+ SUM(price) sm,
+ AVG(price) av,
+ COUNT(price) cn,
+ COUNT(*) AS cna
+ FROM product
+ GROUP BY launch_dt
+ ORDER BY launch_dt")
    launch_dt   ma   mi   sm    av cn cna
1              <NA> <NA> <NA> <NA>  0   1
2  2017-01-29   15   15   30  15.0  2   2
3  2017-01-30   30   25   55  27.5  2   2
4  2017-01-31   10   10   10  10.0  1   1
```

You can group by more than one column. If you do that, rows having the same value on all the columns will form a group.

The following example groups the rows by price and launch date. Even though the Screw and Super_Nut have the same price, they have different launch dates, and therefore form different groups.

```
> sqldf("SELECT price, launch_dt,
+ MAX(price) ma,
+ MIN(price) mi,
+ SUM(price) sm,
+ AVG(price) av,
+ COUNT(price) cn,
+ COUNT(*) AS cna
+ FROM product
+ GROUP BY price, launch_dt
+ ORDER BY price, launch_dt")
  price launch_dt   ma   mi   sm    av cn cna
1    NA              <NA> <NA> <NA> <NA>  0   1
2    10 2017-01-31   10   10   10  10.0  1   1
3    15 2017-01-29   15   15   30  15.0  2   2
4    25 2017-01-30   25   25   25  25.0  1   1
5    30 2017-01-30   30   30   30  30.0  1   1
```

## HAVING Keyword

While a WHERE condition is used to select individual rows, the HAVING condition is used for selecting individual groups. Only groups that satisfy the condition in the HAVING clause will be returned by the query. In other words, the HAVING condition is on the aggregate, not on a column.

If present, the HAVING clause must appear after the GROUP BY, as in the following syntax.

```
SELECT columns,
  aggregate_function(group_columns)
FROM dataframe
WHERE condition
GROUP BY group_columns
HAVING aggregate_condition
ORDER BY columns
```

The following query uses the HAVING condition. Only groups having more than one row (satisfying the COUNT(price) > 1 condition) will be returned. Only one row will be returned, the one with price = 15 and launch date = 29-MAR-17.

```
> sqldf("SELECT price, launch_dt,
+ MAX(price) ma,
+ MIN(price) mi,
+ SUM(price) sm,
+ AVG(price) av,
+ COUNT(price) cn,
+ COUNT(*) AS cna
+ FROM product
+ GROUP BY price, launch_dt HAVING COUNT(price) > 1
+ ORDER BY price, launch_dt")

  price launch_dt ma mi sm av cn cna
1    15 2017-01-29 15 15 30 15  2   2
```

If a WHERE clause is present, it must appear after the GROUP BY clause. Individual rows will be selected by the WHERE condition first before grouping occurs.

```
> sqldf("SELECT price, launch_dt,
+ MAX(price) ma,
+ MIN(price) mi,
+ SUM(price) sm,
+ AVG(price) av,
+ COUNT(price) cn,
+ COUNT(*) AS cna
+ FROM product WHERE p_name NOT IN('Screw', 'New
      Nut')
+ GROUP BY price HAVING COUNT(price) > 1
+ ORDER BY price")
```

Applying aggregate as a WHERE condition clause is not allowed. The following query will give you this error message.

```
> sqldf("SELECT price, launch_dt,
+ MAX(price) ma,
+ MIN(price) mi,
+ SUM(price) sm,
+ AVG(price) av,
+ COUNT(price) cn,
+ COUNT(*) AS cna
+ FROM product
+       WHERE COUNT(price) > 1
+ GROUP BY price HAVING COUNT(price) > 1
+ ORDER BY price")

Error in sqliteSendQuery(con, statement, bind.data) :
  error in statement: misuse of aggregate: COUNT()
```

## Chapter 4: Joining Multiple Data Frames

You can get a subset data frame from more than one data frames. What you do is joining the data frames in your SELECT query.

The syntax for the JOIN is as follows. As you can see from the syntax, you join two data frames on their common columns.

```
SELECT columns FROM dataframe_1 JOIN dataframe_2
ON dataframe_1.column_1 = dataframe_2.column_2
JOIN ... dataframe_n
ON dataframe_2.column_2 = dataframe_n.column_n
WHERE ...
```

Let's say we have the following three data frames in our workspace: c_order (customer order), customer, and product.

```
> c_order

  c_no p_code qty  order_dt
1  10      1 100 2017-04-01
2  10      2 100 2017-04-01
3  20      1 200 2017-04-01
4  30      3 300 2017-04-02
5  40      4 400 2017-04-02
6  40      5 400 2017-04-02

> customer

  c_no         c_name
1   10 Standard Store
2   20  Quality Store
3   30    Head Office
4   40    Super Agent
```

```
> product

  p_code    p_name launch_dt price
1      1      Nail 2017-01-31    10
2      2    Washer 2017-01-29    15
3      3       Nut 2017-01-29    15
4      4     Screw 2017-01-30    25
5      5 Super_Nut 2017-01-30    30
6      6   New Nut              NA
```

Invoking the following sqldf joins the c_order data frame to the customer data frame. The common columns are the c_no.

### Note that:
1. The common columns do not need to have the same name, but they must have the same data type.
2. Columns that have the same name must be qualified by their data frames using dot notation to make sure the data frame the column you are referring to belong to e.g. the c_order.c_no refers to the c_no column of the c_order data frame. See also Data Frame Aliases section below.

```
> sqldf("SELECT c_name,
+    p_code, c_order.qty, c_order.order_dt
+       FROM c_order JOIN customer
+       ON c_order.c_no = customer.c_no ")

         c_name p_code qty   order_dt
1 Standard Store      1 100 2017-04-01
2 Standard Store      2 100 2017-04-01
3  Quality Store      1 200 2017-04-01
4    Head Office      3 300 2017-04-02
5    Super Agent      4 400 2017-04-02
6    Super Agent      5 400 2017-04-02
```

## Data Frame Aliases

In a join query, different data frames can have columns with identical names. To make sure you refer to the correct column of a data frame, you need to qualify it with its data frame. In the previous example, c_order.c_no (the c_no column of the c_order data frame) and customer.c_no (the c_no column of the customer_data frame) were how the c_no columns were qualified. You can set aliases shorter than names of the data frames, a convenient way to qualify columns, which I personally do all the times even for unique columns among the data frames.

In the following example, o is an alias for the c_order data frame and c is an alias for the customer data frame. These aliases are then used in the ON clause to qualify the c_no columns with their respective data frames.

```
> sqldf("SELECT c_name,
+     p_code,
+         o.qty,
+         o.order_dt
+     FROM c_order o
+     JOIN customer c
+     ON o.c_no = c.c_no ")
          c_name p_code qty   order_dt
1 Standard Store      1 100 2017-04-01
2 Standard Store      2 100 2017-04-01
3  Quality Store      1 200 2017-04-01
4    Head Office      3 300 2017-04-02
5    Super Agent      4 400 2017-04-02
6    Super Agent      5 400 2017-04-02
```

The following is an example of joining three data frames.

```
> sqldf("SELECT c_name,
+        p_name,
+        o.qty,
+        o.order_dt
+        FROM c_order o
+        JOIN customer c
+        ON o.c_no = c.c_no
+        JOIN product p
+        ON o.p_code = p.p_code ")

         c_name      p_name qty    order_dt
1 Standard Store       Nail 100 2017-04-01
2 Standard Store     Washer 100 2017-04-01
3  Quality Store       Nail 200 2017-04-01
4    Head Office        Nut 300 2017-04-02
5    Super Agent      Screw 400 2017-04-02
6    Super Agent  Super_Nut 400 2017-04-02
```

## Joining on More than One Column

The preceding joins were on one column. Data frames might need to be joined on more than one column. Here is an example.

Suppose we also have the following shipment data frame.

```
> shipment

  c_no p_code   order_dt shp_qty     ship_dt
1   10      1 2017-04-01      50 2017-04-02
2   10      2 2017-04-01     100 2017-04-02
3   20      1 2017-04-01     100 2017-04-02
4   30      3 2017-04-02     300 2017-04-03
5   10      1 2017-04-01      50 2017-04-10
```

In the following query we join the shipment data frame to the c_order data frame on three columns.

```
> sqldf("SELECT o.c_no,
+         o.p_code,
+            o.order_dt,
+            ship_qty,
+            ship_dt,
+            qty
+         FROM shipment s
+         JOIN c_order o
+         ON s.c_no       = o.c_no
+         AND s.p_code    = o.p_code
+         AND s.order_dt  = o.order_dt ")
  c_no p_code  order_dt ship_qty    ship_dt qty
1   10      1 2017-04-01       50 2017-04-02 100
2   10      2 2017-04-01      100 2017-04-02 100
3   20      1 2017-04-01      100 2017-04-02 200
4   30      3 2017-04-02      300 2017-04-03 300
5   10      1 2017-04-01       50 2017-04-10 100
```

## Left Outer Joins

All the joins so far were inner joins. There is another type of join, the outer join. While an inner join query produces only related rows from the joined data frames, an outer join query produces all rows from one data frame even when some of the rows do not have matching rows from the other data frame.

All rows from the data frame on the left of the left outer join will be in the output whether or not there are matching rows from the data frame on its right. The syntax for the left outer join is as follows.

```
SELECT columns
FROM dataframe_1 LEFT OUTER JOIN dataframe_2
ON dataframe_1.column_1 = dataframe_2.column_2 ...
```

Here's an example left outer join. This query returns all rows from the c_order data frame though its two last rows do not have any matching rows from the shipment data frame.

```
> sqldf("SELECT o.*,
+         ship_dt
+         FROM c_order o
+         LEFT OUTER JOIN shipment s
+         ON o.p_code = s.p_code
+         AND o.c_no  = s.c_no ")
  c_no p_code qty order_dt   ship_dt
1   10      1 100 2017-04-01 2017-04-02
2   10      1 100 2017-04-01 2017-04-10
3   10      2 100 2017-04-01 2017-04-02
4   20      1 200 2017-04-01 2017-04-02
5   30      3 300 2017-04-02 2017-04-03
6   40      4 400 2017-04-02       <NA>
7   40      5 400 2017-04-02       <NA>
```

## Absence of rows in one of data frames

When there is no right-side row to join, the LEFT OUTER JOIN still gives us rows from the left-side data frame.

In our example, if we want to query only orders that have not been shipped at all, we have to put this "only" condition in the WHERE clause. In our case "have not been shipped" means ship_dt IS NULL.

```
> sqldf("SELECT o.*,
+         ship_dt
+         FROM c_order o
+         LEFT OUTER JOIN shipment s
+         ON o.p_code = s.p_code
+         AND o.c_no  = s.c_no
+         WHERE s.ship_dt IS NULL ")
  c_no p_code qty order_dt   ship_dt
1   40      4 400 2017-04-02    <NA>
2   40      5 400 2017-04-02    <NA>
```

## Self-Joins

Assuming some of our products have substitutes. In the following product data frame only the Nut has substitute having the s_code = 5 (the s_code contains the substitute product code) the other products do not have substitutes, their s_code columns are empty (NA).

```
> product

  p_code    p_name  launch_dt  price s_code
1      1      Nail 2017-01-31     10     NA
2      2    Washer 2017-01-29     15     NA
3      3       Nut 2017-01-29     15      5
4      4     Screw 2017-01-30     25     NA
5      5 Super_Nut 2017-01-30     30     NA
6      6   New Nut                NA     NA
```

If you need to know the product name of a substitute, you need a query that joins the product data frame to itself. This kind of join is called a self-join.

Here's how to get the substitute name.

```
> sqldf("SELECT prod.p_code,
+    prod.p_name,
+       subst.p_code subst_p_code,
+       subst.p_name subst_name
+       FROM product prod
+       LEFT OUTER JOIN product subst
+       ON prod.s_code = subst.p_code
+       ORDER BY prod.p_code ")

  p_code    p_name subst_p_code subst_name
1      1      Nail           NA       <NA>
2      2    Washer           NA       <NA>
3      3       Nut            5  Super_Nut
4      4     Screw           NA       <NA>
5      5 Super_Nut           NA       <NA>
6      6   New Nut           NA       <NA>
```

## Natural Joins

If two data frames have columns that share a name, you can naturally join the two data frames on these columns. In a natural join, you do not need to specify the columns that the join should use.

Here's an example. Note the NATURAL JOIN that naturally joins c_order to customer on their common c_no columns.

```
> sqldf("SELECT * FROM c_order NATURAL JOIN
        customer")

  c_no p_code qty order_dt        c_name
1   10      1 100 2017-04-01 Standard Store
2   10      2 100 2017-04-01 Standard Store
3   20      1 200 2017-04-01  Quality Store
4   30      3 300 2017-04-02    Head Office
5   40      4 400 2017-04-02    Super Agent
6   40      5 400 2017-04-02    Super Agent
```

## USING Keyword

A natural join will use all columns with the same names from the joined data frames. If you want your query to join only on some of these identically named columns, instead of using the NATURAL keyword, use the USING keyword.

Here is an example. The c_order data frame join the shipment data frame only on their p_code columns, not on their c_no columns.

```
> sqldf("SELECT p_code, SUM(s.ship_qty)
+       FROM c_order o
+       JOIN shipment s USING (p_code)
+       GROUP BY p_code ")

  p_code SUM(s.ship_qty)
1      1             400
2      2             100
3      3             300
```

## Note

You can manipulate, group/aggregate columns and rows of the output data frame from multiple data frames similar to you do on the output columns and rows from a single data frame, which you learn the previous chapters.

## Chapter 5: Merging Output Data Frames

In the previous Chapter 4 you joined two or more data frames to pick up columns not available in a data frame from another data frame. In this chapter you will learn how to merge rows of the same columns from multiple output data frames. An output data frame is the result of a SELECT statement (a query.

You merge output data frames using UNION ALL, UNION, INTERSECT, or EXCEPT operator. The number of output columns from all queries must be the same and the corresponding columns must have identical or compatible data types.

Assume we have the following product and c_order data frames.

```
> product

  p_code    p_name  launch_dt price s_code
1      1      Nail 2017-01-31    10     NA
2      2    Washer 2017-01-29    15     NA
3      3       Nut 2017-01-29    15      5
4      4     Screw 2017-01-30    25     NA
5      5 Super_Nut 2017-01-30    30     NA
6      6   New Nut                NA    NA

> c_order

  c_no p_code qty   order_dt
1   10      1 100 2017-04-01
2   10      2 100 2017-04-01
3   20      1 200 2017-04-01
4   30      3 300 2017-04-02
5   40      4 400 2017-04-02
6   40      5 400 2017-04-02
```

## UNION ALL

UNION ALL merges all output rows from all the individual queries. Here is an example of UNION ALL. Note that we have two Nail rows as the "FIRST QUERY" and "SECOND QUERY" output columns are "manufactured" output columns to identify the output rows from the first query and second query.

```
> sqldf("SELECT p_code, p_name, 'FIRST QUERY' query
+ FROM product p WHERE p_name LIKE '%Nut%'
+      UNION ALL
+      SELECT p.p_code,
+      p_name,
+      'SECOND_QUERY' query
+      FROM c_order o
+      INNER JOIN product p
+      ON o.p_code = p.p_code ")

  p_code    p_name         query
1      3       Nut   FIRST QUERY
2      5 Super_Nut   FIRST QUERY
3      6   New Nut   FIRST QUERY
4      1      Nail  SECOND_QUERY
5      2    Washer  SECOND_QUERY
6      1      Nail  SECOND_QUERY
7      3       Nut  SECOND_QUERY
8      4     Screw  SECOND_QUERY
9      5 Super_Nut  SECOND_QUERY
```

## UNION

While UNION ALL merges all rows regardless the duplicates, UNION leaves only one of duplicate rows in the final output. Here is an example UNION. Note that we only have one Nail row as the

```
> sqldf("SELECT p_code, p_name, 'FIRST QUERY' query
+ FROM product p WHERE p_name LIKE '%Nut%'
+       UNION
+       SELECT p.p_code,
+       p_name,
+       'SECOND_QUERY' query
+       FROM c_order o
+       INNER JOIN product p
+       ON o.p_code = p.p_code ")

  p_code    p_name         query
1      1      Nail  SECOND_QUERY
2      2    Washer  SECOND_QUERY
3      3       Nut   FIRST_QUERY
4      3       Nut  SECOND_QUERY
5      4     Screw  SECOND_QUERY
6      5 Super_Nut   FIRST_QUERY
7      5 Super_Nut  SECOND_QUERY
8      6   New Nut   FIRST_QUERY
```

## INTERSECT

If you INTERSECT data frames, the merged output rows are only rows that are in all data frames. Next is an example of INTERSECT. The first query produces only two rows. Although the second query produces more product rows, the final output are rows that are in both output.

```
> sqldf("SELECT p_code,
+    p_name
+       FROM product p
+       WHERE p_name LIKE '%Nut%'
+       INTERSECT
+       SELECT p.p_code,
+       p_name
+       FROM c_order o
+       INNER JOIN product p
+       ON o.p_code = p.p_code
+       ORDER BY p_code ")

  p_code    p_name
1      3       Nut
2      5 Super_Nut
```

## EXCEPT

When you combine two SELECT statements using the EXCEPT operator, the final output will be rows from the first query that are not returned by the second query. In the following example, the first query returns all products the second query, only Nuts products, hence the final output rows are only non Nuts products.

```
> sqldf("SELECT p_code, p_name FROM product p
+       EXCEPT
+       SELECT p_code, p_name FROM product WHERE
        p_name LIKE '%Nut%' ")

  p_code p_name
1      1   Nail
2      2 Washer
3      4  Screw
```

## Chapter 6: Built-in Functions

We have used several SQLite built-in (supplied) functions, e.g. DATE and UPPER. These are SQL functions. Don't confuse these SQL functions with the R functions.

SQL functions help you easier in manipulating data. In this chapter, you will see examples of the use of some of the other SQLite built-in functions. Please consult the SQLite documentation for other built-in functions.

### Numeric Functions

### ABS

ABS($n$) returns the absolute value of $n$. For example, the following query returns the absolute value of (price - 20.00) as the third column.

```
sqldf("SELECT p_code, price, (price - 20), ABS(price
     - 20.00) FROM product ")

  p_code price (price - 20) ABS(price - 20.00)
1      1    10           -10                10
2      2    15            -5                 5
3      3    15            -5                 5
4      4    25             5                 5
5      5    30            10                10
6      6    NA            NA                NA
```

### ROUND

ROUND($n$, $d$) returns a number rounded to a certain number of decimal places. The argument $n$ is the number to be rounded and $d$ the number of decimal places. For example, the following query uses ROUND to round price to one decimal place.

Assume our product data frame has the following prices.

```
> product
```

```
  p_code    p_name   launch_dt    price  s_code
1      1      Nail  2017-01-31   10.060      NA
2      2    Washer  2017-01-29   15.110      NA
3      3       Nut  2017-01-29   15.000   5.666
4      4     Screw  2017-01-30   25.505      NA
5      5 Super_Nut  2017-01-30   30.001      NA
6      6   New Nut                   NA      NA
```

Here's to demonstrate the use of the ROUND function, which rounds the price to one decimal.

```
> sqldf("SELECT p_code, price, ROUND (price, 1) FROM
     product ")
```

```
  p_code  price ROUND (price, 1)
1      1 10.060              10.1
2      2 15.110              15.1
3      3 15.000              15.0
4      4 25.505              25.5
5      5 30.001              30.0
6      6     NA                NA
```

## SIGN

SIGN(*n*) returns a value indicating the sign of n. This function returns -1 for *n* < 0, 0 for *n* = 0, and 1 for *n* > 0.

```
> sqldf("SELECT p_code, price, SIGN(price - 15) FROM
     product ")
```

```
  p_code  price SIGN(price - 15)
1      1 10.060               -1
2      2 15.110                1
3      3 15.000                0
4      4 25.505                1
5      5 30.001                1
6      6     NA               NA
```

## Character Functions

### SUBSTR

SUBSTR(*str*, *start_position*, [*length*]) returns a substring of *str* starting from the position indicated by *start_position*. If *length* is not specified, the function returns a substring from *start_position* to the last character in *str*. If *length* is present, the function returns a substring which is *length* characters long starting from *start_position*. If *length* is less than 1, the function returns an empty string.

Suppose you have a customer data frame with the following rows.

```
> customer
  c_no      c_name           phone
1   10 Standard Store 1-416-223-4455
2   20  Quality Store 1-647-333-5566
3   30    Head Office 1-416-111-2222
4   40    Super Agent 1-226-777-8888
```

You want a subset of the phone numbers only. Use the SUBSTR function to solve.

```
> sqldf("SELECT SUBSTR(phone, 7) FROM customer ")

  SUBSTR(phone, 7)
1         223-4455
2         333-5566
3         111-2222
4         777-8888
```

### LOWER and UPPER

LOWER(*str*) converts *str* to lowercase and UPPER(*str*) converts *str* to uppercase. For example, the following query uses LOWER and UPPER. (You have seen the use of UPPER in earlier chapters)

```
> sqldf("SELECT p_name, LOWER(p_name), UPPER(p_name)
        FROM product "
)

  p_name LOWER(p_name) UPPER(p_name)
1    Nail          nail          NAIL
2  Washer        washer        WASHER
3     Nut           nut           NUT
4   Screw         screw         SCREW
5 Super_Nut   super_nut     SUPER_NUT
6  New_Nut      new_nut       NEW_NUT
```

## LENGTH

LENGTH(*str*) returns the length of string *str*. The length of a string is the number of characters in it. For example, the following query returns the length of p_name as the second column.

```
> sqldf("SELECT p_name, LENGTH(p_name) FROM product")

   p_name LENGTH(p_name)
1    Nail              4
2  Washer              6
3     Nut              3
4   Screw              5
5 Super_Nut            9
6  New_Nut             7
```

## Datetime Functions

The following are some of the more important datetime functions. You have seen the use of the DATE function previously. Here is one more, CURRENT_DATE.

## CURRENT_DATE

CURRENT_DATE() returns the current date (the current date of the Oracle server at the time you run the query). For instance, the following query

```
> sqldf("SELECT p_code, launch_dt, CURRENT_DATE FROM
    product ")

  p_code launch_dt CURRENT_DATE
1      1 2017-01-31   2017-01-17
2      2 2017-01-29   2017-01-17
3      3 2017-01-29   2017-01-17
4      4 2017-01-30   2017-01-17
5      5 2017-01-30   2017-01-17
6      6              2017-01-17
```

## Null related functions

# COALESCE

COALESCE(*expr-1*, *expr-2*, ..., *expr-n*) returns the first expression from the list that is not NULL.

Suppose we the following product data frame.

```
> product

  p_code    p_name launch_dt price min_price,
1      1      Nail 2017-01-31    10         NA
2      2    Washer 2017-01-29    15         NA
3      3       Nut 2017-01-29    15         12
4      4     Screw 2017-01-30    20         17
5      5   New Nut 2017-01-30    NA         10
6      6 Newer Nut                NA         NA
```

and you want to get a subset with the sale_price column of the products using this formula:

- If price is available (not NULL) then discount it by 10%
- If price is not available then return min_price
- If both price and min_price are not available, return 5.0

You can use COALESCE to produce the correct sale_price values:

```
> sqldf("SELECT p_name, price, min_price,
+ COALESCE((price * 0.9), min_price, 5.0) sale_price
+      FROM product ")

    p_name price min_price sale_price
1     Nail    10        NA        9.0
2   Washer    15        NA       13.5
3      Nut    15        12       13.5
4    Screw    20        17       18.0
5  New Nut    NA        10       10.0
6 Newer Nut  NA        NA        5.0
```

## NULLIF

NULLIF (*expr1*, *expr2*) compares *expr1* and *expr2*. If they are equal, the function returns null. If they are not equal, the function returns *expr1*.

Suppose you store product old prices in a data frame named old_price. The following old_price data frame, for example, shows two old prices of the Nut product, the products with p_code = 3.

```
> old_product

  p_code    p_name  launch_dt price
1      3       Nut 2016-01-29    15
2      3 Newer Nut 2016-01-29    12
```

Assume our product data frame is as follows.

```
> product

  p_code     p_name  launch_dt price
1      1       Nail 2017-01-31    10
2      2     Washer 2017-01-29    15
3      3 Better Nut 2017-01-29    10
4      4      Screw 2017-01-30    15
```

Let's say you want a subset data frame of the old products with their current price. The following query that employs the NULLIF function gives you the subset.

```
> sqldf("SELECT op.p_code,
+    op.p_name,
+         NULLIF(p.price, op.price) current_price
+         FROM product p
+         JOIN old_product op USING (p_code) ")

  p_code   p_name current_price
1      3 Newer Nut            10
2      3       Nut            10
```

## Chapter 7: Oracle Database

To use the SQL engine to execute your SQL statements, you need to connect to an Oracle database.

Here is an example how I use the **ROracle** package to connect to my localhost Oracle database.

```
> host <- "localhost"
> port <- 1521
> sid <- "XE"
> connect.string <- paste(
+     "(DESCRIPTION=",
+     "(ADDRESS=(PROTOCOL=tcp)(HOST=", host,
      ")(PORT=", port, "))",
+     "(CONNECT_DATA=(SID=", sid, ")))", sep = "")
```

You need to install the ROracle package before loading it into the workspace.

```
> library(ROracle)

> drv <- dbDriver("Oracle")
> con <- dbConnect(drv, username = "djoni", password
        = "grotto007", dbname = connect.string)

> library(sqldf)
```

## Create Data Frame from Database

Assume we have an inventory table in the Oracle database. We can retrieve the inventory data to create a data frame in our R workspace.

```
>   inventory <- sqldf("SELECT * FROM inventory ",
        connection = con)
```

We now have the inventory data frame.

```
> inventory
```

```
  WHS_NO P_CODE WHS_QTY
1      1      1    3000
2      1      2    3500
3      1      3    4000
4      1      4    4500
5      2      1    5000
6      2      2    5500
7      2      6    6000
8      2      7    6500
```

## Full Outer Joins

Full outer join is not supported by RSQLite. You will learn here about full outer join and get it executed by Oracle database.

When you full outer join two data frames, all rows that match and not match will all be returned by the query. Here's an example.

```
> c_order

  c_no p_code qty   order_dt
1   10      1 100 2017-04-01
2   10      2 100 2017-04-01
3   20      1 200 2017-04-01
4   30      3 300 2017-04-02
5   40      4 400 2017-04-02
6   40      5 400 2017-04-02

> inventory

  WHS_NO P_CODE WHS_QTY
1      1      1    3000
2      1      2    3500
3      1      3    4000
4      1      4    4500
5      2      1    5000
6      2      2    5500
7      2      6    6000
8      2      7    6500
```

We full outer join our inventory data frame to c_order data frame. As c_order data frame does not p_code 6 and 7, their columns from the c_order are NA. On the other hand inventory does not have p_code 5, hence its inventory columns are NA.

```
> sqldf("SELECT * FROM c_order FULL OUTER JOIN
        inventory USING(p_code) ", connection = con)

   P_CODE C_NO QTY    ORDER_DT WHS_NO WHS_QTY
1       1    1  20 200 2017-04-01      1    3000
2       1    1  10 100 2017-04-01      1    3000
3       1    2  10 100 2017-04-01      1    3500
4       1    3  30 300 2017-04-02      1    4000
5       1    4  40 400 2017-04-02      1    4500
6       1    1  20 200 2017-04-01      2    5000
7       1    1  10 100 2017-04-01      2    5000
8       1    2  10 100 2017-04-01      2    5500
9       6       NA  NA       <NA>      2    6000
10      7       NA  NA       <NA>      2    6500
11      5       40 400 2017-04-02     NA      NA
```

## STDDEV Function

You can use STDDEV function in Oracle database. STDDEV function, which computes standard deviation, is not supported by SQLite.

```
> sqldf("SELECT whs_no, STDDEV(whs_qty) sdwq FROM
        inventory GROUP BY whs_no", connection = con)

WHS_NO SDWQ
1      645.4972243679028141965442332970666601806
2      645.4972243679028141965442332970666601806
```

## Analytics Windowing

Oracle database has a rich set of analytics windowing functions.

Here is an example of calculating the cumulative average of qty. The calculation is by p_code, i.e. every p_code has its own caq.

```
> c_order

  c_no p_code qty  order_dt
1  10      1 100 2017-04-01
2  10      2 100 2017-04-01
3  20      1 200 2017-04-01
4  30      3 300 2017-04-02
5  40      4 400 2017-04-02
6  40      5 400 2017-04-02

> sqldf("SELECT p_code,
+         AVG(qty) OVER(partition by p_code
+         ORDER BY p_code
+         RANGE BETWEEN UNBOUNDED PRECEDING AND CURRENT
          ROW
+         ) caq
+         FROM c_order ", connection = con)

p_code caq
1      150
1      150
2      300
3      250
4      500
4      500
```

## DML Statements

You can additionally run DML statements: INSERT, UPDATE, and DELETE. These statements must be followed by a SELECT statement.

Let's say we the following customer table.

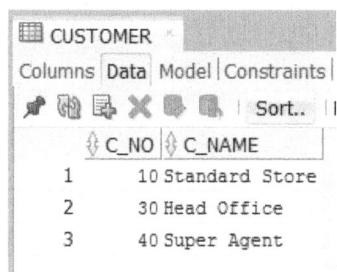

The following statement inserts a new customer and commits the change. Note that the sqldf function takes only one SQL statement argument, hence you need to get multiple statements together into a vector.

```
> sqldf(c("INSERT INTO customer VALUES(1,'New
    Customer')","COMMIT", "SELECT * FROM
    customer") , connection = con)

  C_NO          C_NAME
1   10   Standard Store
2   30      Head Office
3   40      Super Agent
4    1     New Customer
```

# Index

## A

Aggregate Functions · 26

## B

BETWEEN Operator · 16
Built-in Functions · 54

## C

CASE expression · 26
Character Functions · 56
Combining the NOT operator · 19
Compound Conditions · 13
connect to an Oracle database · 62
Create Data Frame from Database · 62

## D

Data Frame Aliases · 41
Database Options · 8
Datetime Functions · 57
DELETE statement · 65
DISTINCT · 23
DML Statements · 65

## E

Escaping the Wildcard Character · 17
Evaluation Precedence · 14
EXCEPT · 53

Expression · 22

## F

Full Outer Joins · 63

## G

G. Grothendieck · 2
GROUP BY · 34
Grouping and Aggregating Rows · 34

## H

Handling NULL · 19
HAVING · 36

## I

IN Operator · 16
In the Set Operators · 64
INSERT statement · 65
INTERSECT · 52

## J

Joining Multiple Data Frames · 40
Joining on More than One Column · 43

## L

Left Outer Joins · 44

LIKE Operator · 17

## M

Manipulating a Data Frame · 22
Merging Output Data Frames · 50

## N

Natural Joins · 46
NOT logical operator · 15
Null related functions · 58
Numeric Functions · 54

## O

Oracle Database · 62
Ordering Output Rows · 29

## R

R Core Team · 2

Renaming Column · 22
**ROracle** · 62

## S

Searched CASE · 28
Selecting All Columns · 12
Selecting Columns · 10
Selecting Rows · 11
Self-Joins · 45
Simple CASE · 26
SQL · 4
sqldf · 4
SQLite · 4
STDDEV Function · 64
**Sub-setting a Data Frame** · 10

## U

UNION · 51
UNION ALL · 51
UPDATE statement · 65
USING Keyword · 47

Made in United States
Orlando, FL
12 May 2023